Rebecca Frederick Lambert

BURIED

PLANTED
THE REVIVAL OF YOU

Harris
House
Publishing

PLANTED
THE REVIVAL OF YOU

Prologue	11
1 | Graveyard of Dreams	13
2 | Broken Faith	20
3 | Precious, Painful Pits	36
4 | Stand Up	43
5 | Grace & Mercy	49
6 | Beautiful Stillness	58
7 | On Purpose	64
8 | Worry for Worship	77
9 | Prepare	89
10 | Planted	101
Epilogue	107

I dedicate this book to each reader or listener. I don't know if someone gave you this book, you were drawn to its theme on your own, or you're part of a small group reading and discussing together. No matter what, my prayer is that through my vulnerability and God's grace you will be renewed in hope, strengthened in joy, and loved into courageously living again!

Foreword

What an honor it is to place this book in your hands.

I had the sacred privilege of watching Rebecca emerge from one of the most painful and stretching seasons of her life. She did so with honesty and humility. I also witnessed her beautiful family walk through that season together—anchored in faith, strengthened by grace, never letting go of hope. What they endured could have buried them. But instead, I saw something different unfold. As Rebecca so humbly shares in the words you are about to read, they were being planted.

Maybe you're carrying a dream you once believed came from God, but it still hasn't come to pass. Maybe you're weighed down by regret over choices you wish you could undo. Or perhaps it's shame—the kind that clings quietly and convinces you that your story no longer qualifies for redemption. If that's where you find yourself, you're not alone. And you're not stuck. There is more.

Rebecca's story is more than inspiring—it's a sacred offering. Her voice is authentic, judgment-free, and rooted in grace. Reading *Planted* feels like sitting with a trusted friend who's not afraid to say, "I've been there," and gently remind you, "You're not buried, friend. You've been planted."

You may have heard the Scripture, "Deep calls to deep . . . " (Psalm 42:7). If you, like me, grew up in Christian circles, you might've heard it quoted in passing and wondered what it really meant. Over the years, I've come to see it as a mysterious yet personal invitation—God's Spirit calling to the deepest parts of who we are. Our hidden longings. Buried dreams. Wounds we're afraid to revisit. But just because something has been buried doesn't mean it's been forgotten. With God, those hidden things are never wasted. They're being nurtured. Transformed. Rooted.

In *Planted*, Rebecca gently uncovers those buried places and shows us how God uses even our most broken chapters to grow something beautiful. Her story reminds us that we are not forgotten in the waiting. We are not disqualified by our detours. In His hands, the soil of disappointment becomes fertile ground for deep roots and good fruit.

So as you turn these pages, let God's love speak life to your soul. I pray that Rebecca's words—soaked in kindness and wisdom—water the dry places of your heart. May this book draw you back to the dreams you once tucked away and the holy calling that may have felt too weighty to hold. Let it remind you that the process you're in has purpose. You're becoming like the tree in Psalm 1—planted by streams of water, steady and strong, bearing fruit in due season.

Let this be the season your roots go deep.

Terry Tamashiro Harris, Publisher
Harris House Publishing | Torch Runner Books
Author of *Love Remains: A Mercy House Novel*

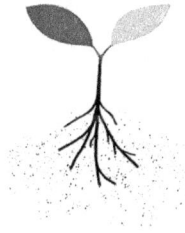

Prologue

I walk between the carefully planned rows of pretty stones, meticulously etched with sweet remembrances of dear memories. I am not alone in this cemetery; others look with me. We stand confused, feeling an overwhelming sense of loss, although we aren't sure what we are mourning. I want to cry, but I'm not sure if I should. Would I appear weak?

The words engraved in stone leave us all dumbfounded. One reads, "gifted doctor"; another "loving missionary," "worshiper," "esteemed artist," "outstanding athlete," "compassionate pastor," "mentor," "generous executive," "inventor," "cultivator," "teacher," "counselor," "visionary." All powerful depictions. Any of them would be a delightful title to carry. Except these words don't belong to someone buried beneath. These descriptive tombstones belong to a living person's dreams. These and a thousand others are hopes and visions for the future that someone has buried; given up on; left for dead.

It's a graveyard of dreams.

Graveyard of Dreams

I know. The opening of this book doesn't exactly
send joyful thoughts through your mind, doesn't give
you the "warm fuzzies," doesn't fill you with hope. I
know. The thought of a graveyard does not carry a
positive connotation for most of us. And the idea of
burying your dreams, your desires for the future, your
great aspirations, plans, and goals? Actually digging
a grave to throw them all into? Well, that's unthink-
able! How appalling to even entertain the idea. I
know. It's terrifying. I know; because I was there. How
many of us have had that suffocating feeling that
we've completely blown it? I was there. I remember
the heaviness, though I'm not willing to ponder it for
long. When you have totally and completely screwed
up, and there is no way you can see to make things
right; when you know that nothing will ever be the

same, that's when it hits. You doom yourself. One by one, those dreams you had as a child are thrown into the hole. It is painful. It seems as if your heart goes in with them. It's hard to breathe. I know. I remember. Part of me was dead. Literally. On the outside, I was still breathing, walking, going through the motions, but on the inside, I was buried alive. I was stuck under the weight of guilt, shame, disgust, condemnation, and self-imposed isolation.

When we bury our dreams, we bury who we are. We deny what we were created for. Not pursuing these dreams makes as little sense as designing and making the world's most advanced, highest-resolution camera and never taking a photograph with it. It's as sad as finding a cure for a world-threatening disease and hiding it in a lab. It just doesn't make sense! But can I be bold and say many (if not most) of us do it?

Planting a Seed

When we bury our **dreams**, we bury who we are. We deny what we were created for.

Imagine with me. What if Thomas Edison had buried his dream? After hundreds of failed attempts to perfect his creation, no one would blame him.

What if Johnny Cash had given into his life of extreme poverty as a child, believing that that was just where he belonged? What if Michael Jordan had allowed his loss of almost 300 games, or the over 9,000 shots he missed to destroy his dream? What if, after being sold by his brothers and being imprisoned, Joseph had stopped believing the dreams that God had given him? What if, with the hundreds of threats looming over him and his loved ones, Dr. Martin Luther King Jr. decided to bury his dream?

What if the dreams that God placed in your heart are the answer to the prayers of others? What if someone's life depends on it?

I believe with all my heart that God especially loves raising up people who are a shattered, unbelievable mess. He is ready to resurrect those dreams if we let Him. It may be a long road ahead. You may feel way too broken, but one thing I know: The God who created you can surely create a YOU 2.0!

The truth is that God is not in any way surprised by the current state of your life. He wasn't shocked when you made that bad decision that you regret to this day. He didn't turn away in disgust or walk away from you. No. He looked at your heart through the lens of Jesus who covers all and reached out His hand to pick you up. He loves you . . . and has known you longer than you've even existed on this earth. Let that little fact sink in.

Look, I don't know where you are right now on your life journey. Maybe you've already taken His hand, and you are struggling through the process of getting back on track . . . whatever that means for you. Or maybe you're still lying in a fetal position, traumatized by the way things turned out. Well, friend: If you are still breathing . . . things haven't actually *turned out* yet! You are not done. There is so much more. Wherever you are, God has plans for you and wants to do real-life miracles in and through you.

Planting a Seed

Wherever you are, God has plans for you and wants to do real-life miracles in and through you.

Others of you reading this book never really had a terrible crash-and-burn moment in life. Maybe so far you're thinking, "Oh good, I'm okay then. I have never felt all *that* before." Well, I'm thankful on your behalf for that, and I celebrate every blessing with you, but in no way does that mean you're off the hook. If you have been able to stand firm in your faith, unwavering in your dreams and desires, you better believe there are hurting, broken people all around you that are desperately waiting for you to step out and help them dig their way out of the darkness that surrounds them. You'll get dirty. It won't be comfortable at all. You will learn more about grace than you ever expected to understand. And you will find the deepest fulfillment as you give yourself away.

Or perhaps you've never given Jesus much thought. The depth of your pain or struggle has made it difficult for you to believe there could be a loving God who created you. Maybe you have been hurt by someone who professed to serve Jesus, and that didn't make sense to you. Some of you have been devastated by a church in the past, and you're still building barriers to protect yourself from further attacks. To you I say, *I am so sorry*. Thank you for giving my words a little room in your broken heart.

So whoever you are, whatever your reality is right now, no matter how deep your hole is or how much dirt is piled on top . . . decide with me that the day has come. Now is the right time to be renewed. Today salvation, restoration, redemption, and healing

17

are available to you with nothing held back. Right now is when some of us need to step out of our comfy corners and give of ourselves like lives *gravely* depend on it.

Are you ready?

I cannot wait to see what God does in and through you. And I'm praying for you now, even as I finish writing this first chapter.

PSALM 119:169–176 (NIV)

May my cry come before you, Lord; give me understanding according to your word. May my supplication come before you; deliver me according to your promise. May my lips overflow with praise, for you teach me your decrees. May my tongue sing of your word, for all your commands are righteous. May your hand be ready to help me, for I have chosen your precepts. I long for your salvation, Lord, and your law gives me delight. Let me live that I may praise you, and may your laws sustain me. I have strayed like a lost sheep. Seek your servant, for I have not forgotten your commands.

DISCUSSION QUESTIONS

1. Can you relate to this chapter? It describes several "places" you might be right now. Which one best describes you?

2. Can you look back and identify any dreams you have buried?

3. What thoughts do you have about the paragraph regarding Thomas Edison, Johnny Cash, Michael Jordan, Joseph, and Dr. Martin Luther King Jr.?

4. This chapter says, "The truth is that God is not in any way surprised by the current state of your life." What do you think about that?

5. Be honest—do you believe God loves you and wants to restore you?

Broken Faith

I know that, for a long time now, God has been preparing me to write this book. And since I believe what the Bible says in Proverbs 16:9 about how we plan what we are going to do, but God is directing our paths, I also know that you are reading this because God wants you to receive this message. How cool is that?!

Something I want to make clear right off the bat is that *me* being the messenger and *you* being the receiver in no way makes me the expert. In fact, I am hearing from the Lord while writing this just as much as I pray you'll hear from Him while you're reading it. I just happen to have lived through some difficulties, challenges, and the results of my own choices , all of which have made me who I am today. And as I have chosen to submit every bit of who I am to the

Lordship of Jesus Christ, He now empowers me to be an authentic, transparent, openly imperfect girl who desperately needs grace. So here we are . . . you and me . . . through this book, because God has directed our paths. I hope you have a sense of excitement about what He wants to do in us.

I grew up in an environment that movies are made of. As a missionary kid (MK) in Argentina, I was surrounded by a move of God that reached thousands upon thousands. I was raised by parents who were spiritual giants in the eyes of many—especially mine and my sisters'. Being the baby of four girls meant having the best hand-me-downs, working hard for all the attention, and looking up to three VIPs my entire life. I remember seeing each of them as completely *perfect*. I thought, "If I can only become like them, I'll be okay." My favorite thing in life was to sing with them and my mommy from the time I was barely old enough to talk. I grew up speaking English at home and Spanish everywhere else, and I somehow knew when to speak each language. I never knew just one, and that was normal.

The only culture I knew was that of Buenos Aires, intermingled with the tidbits of American culture that my daddy shared with us. This consisted of country music videos that my uncle would send us, knowledge of the Dodgers, and even some OU football mixed in. My mom was more Latin American than anything else, since she was also an MK growing up in Honduras. We all fit right in, and there was never a thought in my mind about ever living elsewhere. I love the beautiful people of Argentina, the *asados* and *empanadas*, the *tango*, drinking *mate* with friends, and of course, soccer. When it's World Cup time, be aware that my family is crazy and loud—and sporting our jerseys, crazy hats, and flags to support Argentina. Ever heard of the G.O.A.T., Lionel Messi?? Yep. Argentine.

My earliest thoughts about what the USA was like involved a mixture of Mickey Mouse, *Back to the Future*, and the voices of Loretta Lynn and Conway Twitty. Not a bad start, I think, but not quite encompassing of real life. When we would visit the States on furlough, we spent most of our time in Los Angeles visiting our church's headquarters, and we'd stay

Planting a Seed
Worship was raw and real and imperfect and full of the love of God

in the "Missionary Home." This was an apartment
building set up for those who, like my parents, were
only in the USA temporarily while serving abroad.
We always got to visit a magical warehouse of sorts
called the "Alabaster House," where we could choose
a new toy, blanket, and other treasures that some
wonderful people had donated for us. I felt extremely
special. It still moves me every time I remember those
experiences.

Life really was wonderful. I loved it. I was a happy
kid. I may have thought I was a princess. I realized later
in life that what made my childhood extremely unique
was the move of God that surrounded me. People
were coming to Jesus in droves, sick people were
receiving healing, hurting people became whole. At
the big meetings, there was always a separate tent or
space where people were being freed from demon
possession. This was "normal life." As a little girl, I'd
play in the back of the church building where I'd line
up dolls, or even my sweet cousins or friends, and I'd
preach to them—this was the world I knew. Worship
was raw and real and imperfect and full of the love of
God. I was at home in His presence. I wanted nothing more than to serve Him forever. It's hard for me

to really put this time into words. It was truly awesome. I'd like to share three stories from that time in Argentina that'll at least give you a glimpse into the way the Holy Spirit was involved in everyday life.

As you know, we didn't use American dollars; of course, online banking didn't exist yet, so mommy (yes, we still call her that) would have to physically take cash downtown to exchange it from time to time. On one of those days, as she took a shortcut from our school to the train station with the money she would exchange, she had to travel a narrow path. She saw two men walking toward her, and as they drew nearer, they linked arms so she wouldn't be able to pass. She began to pray in the Spirit under her breath and continued walking. Suddenly, the men stopped dead in their tracks, looked behind my mother wide-eyed, and turned away and ran until they were out of sight. No, she didn't see anything behind her. What did they see? She later learned that there had been many hold-ups recently in that very spot, and was thankful for the protectors that the Lord sent.

The next situation is about me at two and a half. I was a bundle of non-stop energy, and on this particular day, I was super excited about ice cream. As

I ran full speed into the parlor, I met head-on with a steel pole. The impact was hard, and I was knocked out cold. I was rushed to the emergency room, where my mom and eldest sister waited for the X-ray results and prayed. The news wasn't good. The doctor communicated that I had fractured my skull. Thankfully, mommy and Brenda weren't okay with accepting that, so they prayed some more and asked them to redo the X-ray. They re-did it, and the fracture was gone.

Allow me to share one more. My daddy traveled quite a bit in Argentina, and many times, he'd minister in Chaco-Formosa, which was to our north. It's home to the Toba Indians, and Daddy loved them so very much. During one of his trips there, he was about to preach when a situation arose. Some of the local people came in carrying a baby; the doctors had told them that the baby was dead, but they had heard about a God who could help. They simply handed the baby to my dad and said, "You pray to God for him so he will come back to life." Daddy honestly had no idea what to do, so he just did as they asked and prayed. The baby started breathing, and then moving, and then began to cry. He handed him back to his mother, and that was that.

Is that incredible to you? As in, literally, do you find these life stories hard to believe? Because that was our normal. That's just how our powerful God works. He moves, He provides, He heals—He is a miraculous God. Are you starting to see why I call my childhood unique?

When I was about to start middle school, my parents heard from the Lord very clearly that it was time to return to their homeland, the USA. I was devastated about the move away from everything I had known; my friends, my church, my school, my home, my culture, my country of birth. I remember crying very quietly on the plane as it pulled away from the terminal at the Ezeiza International Airport in Buenos Aires. I knew I was mad, but I had no idea about the culture shock that awaited me.

Ada, Oklahoma. Ever heard of it? My guess is that most of you have not. It is a small town in southeastern Oklahoma of around 17,000 people and is home to the Chickasaw Nation. I would spend the next twelve years of my life there, and although I look back now on some very sweet memories with some of the kindest human beings on earth, it was not an easy transition. In fact, "not easy" is a gross understatement.

It is very hard for me to put into words what I experienced in the first few years in Ada. Some of it is a blur. I definitely felt like we had moved to the middle of nowhere, and I'm not gonna lie—I was disappointed. I couldn't understand why my incredible parents left

Planting a Seed

The doctors had told them that the baby was dead, but they had heard about a God who could help.

such a thriving ministry to come to a desolate place to plant a church with six people in attendance.

Within the first couple of months there, the house we were living in with dear friends-turned-family burned, leaving only the slab behind. I couldn't have told you at that age, but looking back now, there are many vivid memories that strike me, leaving me to realize it was a traumatic event for me. We were thankful that the barrels of belongings that were coming in a shipment from Argentina hadn't yet arrived, but the loss was still devastating. I found consolation in my caring teachers and administrators, making school a safe place for me. I also found out just how kind, compassionate, and generous our new community was; a gymnasium was set up with a section for each of us. People brought clothes and other things

27

and, we were not left with any unmet needs.

This event was a fast-forward moment for acclimating to Ada. I hadn't known what to expect from *any* aspect of life. I made a few friends and eventually got used to American public school, which led to more friends. I rapidly went from a very awkward missionary kid from South America to a pretty normal teenager trying to find her way through the weirdest stage of life (that's the one way I was actually *like* everyone around me in middle school).

I guess I should tell you that I love music and have enjoyed singing in front of a crowd since I was very little, and have always felt right at home on a stage. I have always been smitten with the fine arts. Even when I was still preschool-aged, my mom would come into the family room in the morning expecting to find me watching cartoons, but I'd be watching operas instead. I had the opportunity to play Young Cosette in the musical *Les Miserables* when I was about six years old, and I was enamored with performing from then on (thank you, Mr. Peter!). As I mentioned earlier, I had heard some classic country music growing up, but after arriving in Oklahoma, I began to enjoy more of it, as well as every genre of

American music in the nineties (don't judge). It didn't take me long to find places to perform in and around Ada, and before long, I was singing pretty often in school, at area opries, rodeos, and ballgames. I also remained involved in leading worship at our church, where I eventually wrote some of the songs we sang to the Lord.

From the outside looking in, I was doing great! A happy, healthy, normal teen (if normal's even possible!). I earned good grades, I was involved in many things at school, I had friends, I was singing, active at church; all good things. However, there were some feelings that I will always struggle to explain that I began to carry with me. I continuously wondered what my life would've been like had we stayed in Buenos Aires. I'd notice how close my classmates were to those they'd grown up with since kindergarten, and I'd long for that. I missed the big revival meetings that had always filled my heart with joy. I'd think about how I could never measure up to my sisters because my opportunities would be so different from theirs. Every time someone asked me where I was actually from, I'd have to explain the country of my birth, and how I'm from Argentina, but I realize I look like I'm from here, but that my heart was more Latina, but my parents are American, even though my mom grew up in Honduras and is more Latina herself . . . it was always complicated and exhausting. People found it fascinating and wonderful, but for some reason, it brought me great pain. I knew I didn't belong. I would never really fit in, *but boy, did I try*.

Of all the things I missed, and still do to this day, it's everything that was tied to ministry and the move of God that I longed for the most. I am not saying that God wasn't moving in my new hometown, but somehow I just couldn't find Him as easily anymore. I never saw or heard about healings, freedom from possession, or other moves of the Holy Spirit . . . In fact, if I brought up anything of that nature, people looked at me funny. I was so confused because I thought I was moving to the American "Bible belt," and it felt like nothing of the sort. It felt very dry. A lot of people had so much, but seemed so empty. I longed to go back *home*. Eventually, I accepted the fact that those years and that reality were behind me. I had been baptized in the Holy Spirit at around nine years old, knowing I could count on His guidance at any given moment, but now I felt alone. I wondered why I didn't see His mighty power or feel His presence the same way anymore. I couldn't hear Him. I was feeling let down. (Spoiler alert: *He* never left *me*.)

That was the season of life when boys became my focus. It was unlikely that you'd find me "single" during my high school days. Looking back now, I see that while having a boyfriend was a typical component of teen life, for me, it was also a distraction from the fact that *I was losing my first love*. Rather than pressing into the Lord and fighting for another experience of *His* love, His power, His glory, I gave up on that and did what all the "normal" kids around me did. I can pretty much correlate each grade in high school with the boys that fit into them. I missed out on so much time with the Lord, so many opportunities to grow, and instead, I became dependent on having a romantic relationship to fill the void. I was disappointed several times.

Planting a Seed

Hear this: The choices you make do not define who you are.

I remember a specific break-up with a boyfriend I had gotten intimately involved with. I was convinced, as teenage girls tend to become, that he would

31

always be mine, and that we had a real thing going. Apparently his perspective on high school love was not nearly as permanent as mine. I was on the front porch, on my knees, begging him not to break up with me. I was so desperate to stay in the relationship, because I had "learned" that the only way to fix this mistake was to stay together and get married. The relationship ended that day, and I was devastated. I thought my front porch interaction with this boy had been private, until I walked back inside, my face tear-stained and red, my lungs sucking air. That's when I realized my daddy had been observing through the front window. He hugged me and said, "Baby, he doesn't get to have your dignity. You are worth more than that." Oof! There were a lot of things going through my young mind in this moment, but the main thing that sticks out today is this: My daddy loved me unconditionally. I wish I had truly realized that a long time ago.

Listen. Find those people whom you can trust with your authentic self; the broken, dirty, yucky self that you are ashamed of. You need to let someone help you separate who you are from something you have done. Shame is a nasty weapon of darkness. It attacks your identity. Hear this: The choices you make do not define who you are. You are created in the image of God. You are more valuable than diamonds or gold. After you've learned that, BE the person others can trust with their authentic self, and then grow from there.

I grew up in a generation that was expected to hide the bad stuff and look shiny and clean on the outside. There was no place for the mistakes. Nobody put this requirement on me; it just was. As a daughter of ministry, this requirement was compounded, and my enemy made sure the secret shame was too. This is the season in which my vibrant, thriving relationship with the Lord turned into a routine I was really good at. I was at church every time the doors opened: Sunday morning, Sunday night, and Wednesday night. And yes, *I still loved Jesus.* And I still sang to Him, an activity that will always be my favorite. Beyond that, I could sure *talk the talk.* From the outside, I know I appeared

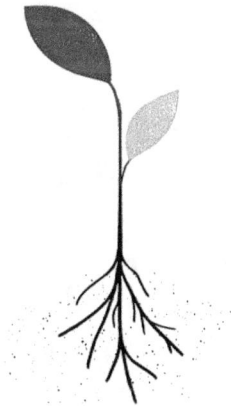

33

to have it all together; but on the inside, I was already cracking—my heart was troubled, and I was struggling with a broken faith.

REVELATION 2:4 (TPT)

But I have this against you: you have abandoned the passionate love you had for me at the beginning.

DISCUSSION QUESTIONS

1. What are some of the best memories you carry from your childhood?

2. Who did you look up to when you were a child and why?

3. Is there a massive change or turning point in your story that has impacted you ever since? How did it change you?

4. Where have you felt at home? What made the place, or places, special to you?

5. Have you ever felt like God was absent? What did you do about that?

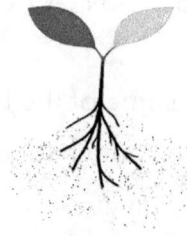

Precious, Painful Pits

Have you ever noticed that when you start "digging a hole," sometimes it's easier to keep digging than to climb out and fill it back in? Why don't we just stop? I have seen it over and over again; as humans, we are just naturally inclined to make mistakes, make messes, and hurt people, especially ourselves and those closest to us, until we find ourselves deep in a pit. Have you ever made a mistake that left you feeling worthless? And then, since you felt like you already messed up so badly, you might as well forget it and just let yourself do whatever you want—even if it's a terrible idea? Have you ever found it much easier to give in to your flesh (your natural human desires) than to give yourself to the Father because you were just way too dirty? If you have, I know your struggle. I know something else too: *The enemy of your soul loved every minute of it.* He was right there whispering lies into your heart, making sure to confirm and exaggerate every negative thought you had about yourself. He made sure you believed everyone was watching you and judging you. He added to your guilt an abundance of shame and crippling anxiety— the kind you try to escape by making irrational decisions that only add to your pain. He certainly made you feel crazy if you considered asking for help, or even more, if you actually dared to ask for forgiveness. Does any of this sound familiar? If so, I want to help you silence that nasty voice and begin listening to the voice of a good Savior who *loves* you, *created* you, wants to *bless* you, who *forgives* you, *does not condemn you*, went all the way to death on a cross just because He wants to stay in relationship with you forever, *no matter what.*

See, in my early twenties, I found myself in that kind of pit. It was during those days that I landed in the darkest point of my life. When I say it was dark . . . I mean that I couldn't see any hope for the future. In fact, I couldn't even plan a few hours ahead. I missed my college graduation ceremony because I was in a hospital on suicide watch. One mistake led to another until I was only twenty-one years old, divorced, alone, having severely let down every single person I cared about. Yes, all of them. The further I had walked in my own ability, talent, and plan, or lack thereof . . . the worse it had gotten. And man, I did it for a long time.

I can say that in my current day, I'm an open book (pun intended), but for those few years leading into my twenties, my cover didn't correlate with the pages inside. The longer you keep your struggles in the dark, the harder it is to expose them. We can look pretty good from the outside, and we can fool everyone around us, but *we cannot fool ourselves or God.* At some point, the show you are putting on will get too exhausting. You can convince yourself that "it's all good" for a while, but your heart can only take so much of that. And as a natural performer, I was good at keeping on . . . but I was tired, empty, and really hurting. Looking back, I feel like the persona I lived out publicly during those years was the one I thought I *should be*, but not who I actually was. Little by little, I suppressed how I really felt, what I really thought, who I really was. If I had only given God more of my attention instead of focusing on myself, He would have taken who I really was, who He created me to be, and led me in love toward the healing I desperately needed. Unfortunately, I didn't leave time for that. I was a runaway train. I was still carrying so much disappointment, but I was determined to pretend everything was fine, I was fine, I was happy, life was good. You can only patch and cover so many cracks until the whole thing comes crumbling down—and crumble I did.

The most devastating part of my pit was letting down my parents and my sisters—and their families. My life pursuit had been of being "like them" when it should've been of following Jesus toward who He made *ME* to be. We all tend to put a lot of effort into impressing the people around us instead of pleasing God. And while I'm being honest, my family had become a sort of idol in my life. I just needed to remain good enough to be a part of it. The way I compared myself to my sisters was so unhealthy, and it was unfair to everyone involved. The reality of being a teen in the nineties in the USA didn't look anything like their reality of being teens in the eighties in Argentina. What seems so obvious now was not even a thought in my mind back then. Of course, I was a kid.

A lot of healing has happened since those days,

and many relationships have been restored to their beauty. But I'm not going to lie to you. At times, I was angry with the people I loved the most. On this side of healing, I realize that some of them didn't know how to navigate this uncharted territory where a family member *very publicly* needed grace. My sins

Planting a Seed

He wants to stay in relationship with you forever, no matter what.

weren't secret, and that was uncomfortable. Have you heard the phrase "hurt people (will) hurt people?" We were in that zone pretty heavily, and I heard some pretty painful things said about me and to me.

If I knew then what I know now, I would've saved myself a LOT of pain. So let me save you some: *Comparison is the thief of joy*. Wait. Read it again, slowly: *Comparison is the thief of joy*. I'm not sure what situation Teddy Roosevelt was in when he coined this phrase, but I do know that if you live your life based on the lives of others, you will lose your very identity. At the bottom of this pit, *I didn't even know who I was*. I had buried my dreams, my hopes, my emotions, my love . . . I was breathing, but I was not alive. How many of us find ourselves there? Please, don't stay there. I know you don't want to.

Underneath the profound pain we were all experiencing was the beginning of the road toward true freedom. The enemy would have preferred that I keep struggling in secret, because that is where he has control and can keep us in the mode of shame, all alone. Now that it was all out in the open that "Rebecca isn't perfect" (insert gasp), the real me could get back to living. There was a long road ahead, but it was the start of a genuine, authentic, raw pursuit of life.

Here's the deal. I have seen what I call an "epidemic of stuck" in so many people around me for so long, and I know there is a way out of it. The world around me is covered in pits, in a graveyard of dreams, some of *your* dreams! I can't let that just be okay. That's why I'm writing this book and that's why I am so glad you are reading it. If you are in any way *stuck in a pit* and not feeling like this is the life God has for you, read on. Whether you're stuck because of shame, fear, or confusion, there is freedom for you. Don't stop here. Let's move!

LUKE 15:21 (NIV/AUTHOR'S PARAPHRASE)

Father, I have sinned against heaven and against you. I am no longer worthy to be called your daughter (or son).

DISCUSSION QUESTIONS

1. This chapter talks about the enemy of your soul, the devil; his plan is to harm you. Did this description of how he lies to you sound familiar? Can you recognize that nasty voice?

2. "We cannot fool ourselves or God." Be honest with yourself. Do people truly know *you*? Or have you been portraying someone you think they *want* to see?

3. Do you ever get exhausted because you are trying to do or be "good enough" for others or for God? Do you need to confess any "secret" sins?

4. Do you tend to compare yourself with others, even if it's those you aspire to be like? How could you change your focus to who *you are* and what *your* purpose is?

5. Are you stuck in a pit you'd like to get out of? Or do you know anyone who is? Have you buried dreams, identity, part of you, and would like to dig it all out?

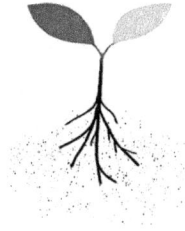

Stand Up

When you stand up in a room where others are sitting, you command attention. Standing is usually the stance when a speaker addresses a crowd of hearers, like a professor lecturing a class of students. Standing is necessary if you're about to walk somewhere. Standing is a relief after sitting in a car for several hours . . . or after you've been down in a painful pit and have decided to climb out. Yours might look different, but my start to restoration involved my need to *stand up* before a church full of people.

I remember Easter Sunday, March 31st, 2002. Through the grace and strength of a God who loves me, I managed to stand on the stage of the church my mom and dad pastored in Ada. Yep, the church where I had served since we arrived many years before—where I had been a youth group member, had led worship, taught Sunday school, and most recently co-led youth. And . . . the same church where I had let everyone down with my humanness. No one asked me to do this. It was not a requirement I bent to. I *chose* to stand on that stage in complete vulnerability. I wept. Boy, that was a hard thing to do. Painful. Oh, so uncomfortable. I shared how deeply sorry I was for the hurt I had caused people, and I asked for their forgiveness. I told them how my parents had shown me unconditional love and that I felt more than ever the love of our Heavenly Father. For the first time, *I understood . . . really understood . . . grace, salvation, and mercy.* Did everyone in that room quickly forgive me and love me without reservation? No. And honestly, I don't blame them. But most of them did exactly that. I leaned on the continued love, prayer, and support of many people in that congregation as I walked my road of healing. And to this day, I love to visit that beautiful place where God met me and gave me another chance to live a life that glorifies Him.

Have you ever questioned whether you really understand grace, salvation, and mercy? If you are like many modern-day "Christians," chances are you do not. I think I know why, based on my personal experience. *We don't understand salvation because we don't understand repentance.* There are a lot of churches today that shy away from topics like repentance, because it just isn't popular; it doesn't exactly draw a crowd, you know?

Repentance is not easy, but it leads to life. Unfortunately, many of us regret our actions and the consequences they bring, but we don't have the hope that leads us to repent. Think about Judas, the disciple who ultimately betrayed Jesus for some coins and turned Him over to His death. We know he was filled with regret, because we see in Matthew 27 that he returned the thirty pieces of silver to the high priests and told them he had betrayed innocent blood. When the priests and elders basically said, "Too bad for you," Judas threw the money into the temple, went away, and hanged himself. Too terrible. He didn't have hope. My heart just breaks for anyone who gets to this place of hopelessness. If that's you right now, please call a loved one. If you don't think you have that, call a helpline (988) or go to a hospital. Nothing is worth ending your life over. Absolutely nothing.

In contrast, when we look at Simon Peter,

another disciple of Jesus, we see that after he disowned Jesus (three times before the rooster crowed), he wept bitterly, but later repented and continued to follow Him. I love that this Simon Peter, the one who failed miserably and needed to repent and be reinstated by Jesus, this is the very one to whom Jesus said, "And I tell you that you are Peter, and on this rock I will build my church, and the gates of Hades will not overcome it" (Matthew 16:18). You know why? Because Peter knew who Jesus was—the Son of God. That gave him the hope he needed to pursue repentance.

Here's the bad news: At some point in your life, you will need to repent, likely many times a day. And that's okay. *The good news?* There is hope, salvation, and redemption for you if you are willing to repent. Stand up! Repent! If it requires someone else to hear it, go to them! Stand up and see what He does for you! *He will blow your mind.*

See, God designed us to feel remorse over our sin so that it would lead us to repentance, which leads to victory over sin. But the enemy will distort your thoughts, your feelings, your remorse, and do all that he can to lead you toward worldly regret. And *that* is where we get stuck. We see no way out of it, so we stay *stuck* and assume our life is just a consequence of our sin with no hope for a better future. STOP LISTENING TO HIM. He is the father of LIES. He is the enemy of your very being!

If you are done living life according to Satan's lies, pray right now. Tell God that you repent of your sins (name any of them you want), and that you know He sent His Son to die and redeem you! Ask Jesus to live within you, to change you, to restore you, and to bring you new life! He cannot wait to get started once you invite Him in. Maybe you accepted Jesus years ago, but your life's fruit is not aligning with that. Repent again. And again, and again. We will never "arrive" on this side of Heaven. That is why His mercies are *new every morning*. NEW! Not the same over and over again—new! This morning, gifts of mercy were sent to cover your needs for today. Before you roll out of bed each morning, accept the mercies He has provided for you. I know I need them every single day.

2 CORINTHIANS 7:10 (NIV)

Godly sorrow brings repentance that leads to salvation and leaves no regret, but worldly sorrow brings death.

DISCUSSION QUESTIONS

1. What do salvation, grace, and mercy mean to you?

2. Is there anything you need to repent of today? Or do you want to do that for the first time and receive Jesus as your Savior?

3. "And I tell you that you are Peter, and on this rock I will build my church, and the gates of Hades will not overcome it." This is the same man who denied Jesus and needed to repent. What does this mean for us?

4. How would you compare worldly regret and actual repentance?

5. His mercies are not the same every morning; they are new. What does this mean for you?

Grace & Mercy

Raise your hand if you have a t-shirt, mug, crafty sign, or even a tattoo with either grace or mercy on it. Okay, if you're too cool for that, I bet you've at least heard a song or two with either of those words in the lyrics. In my high school days, we loved listening to old tunes recorded by The Judds . . . and one of my favorites was "Have Mercy." (Not exactly the kind I'm referring to.) Grace and mercy are great examples of words that we tend to use pretty lightly; if we aren't careful, the weight of their meaning can be lost in the shuffle.

Mercy is defined as the withholding of appropriate consequences or punishment. The appropriate consequence for sin is death, but the God of mercy doesn't want that for you or me. That's why He sent Jesus. That's mercy. *Grace* is the spontaneous, unmerited gift of divine favor in the salvation of sinners, and the divine influence operating in individuals for their regeneration and sanctification. If you and I are going to rise out of our pits and into a beautiful, thriving life, we need both grace and mercy. BEST NEWS EVER: They are both available! Right now!

I have seen both of these divine gifts at work in my life over and over. Beyond salvation and eternal life with Jesus, which would be more than enough, I've seen His hand on my life in ways that blow my mind. When you make the choice to live for Him, follow His will, and submit to His ways, the treasure trove is endless.

I see mercy when I approach the throne room with my daily mistakes and ask for forgiveness. He gives it freely. His mercy has provided protection, a refuge for my soul. His mercy makes Him patient with me as I learn. His mercy has been poured out on us since the beginning of time. The mercy of God opens the door of Heaven to me and to you!

I see grace when I look at my husband. I have often called him my biggest gift of grace on this earth. That's because I know I don't deserve the gift of our beautiful marriage and God's unmerited favor that brought this man to me. I was still so broken when I met Jesse, and after he and I made the decision and commitment to pursue God throughout our relationship, God used him to support me in my healing (and used me to help him, too)! That's grace. Grace is getting to watch Jesse come from a background unlikely to lead and then step into his ministry calling with rare humility and sincere love for the people he meets.

I have seen grace when my two sons raise their voices in worship to Jesus. I've seen it when I am able to counsel a child or an adult who is struggling, and they find peace. When a person crippled with anxiety finds rest. When provision comes in like a flood time and time again. When I am with my extended family, and we reflect on His blessings, the legacy, the promises. When I wake up to the shining sun. When I hear birds sing or watch them fly. When I lie down on soft grass and look up into the beautiful night sky. When my feet crunch on sand or snow. When I get lost in a song (or ten) to Jesus.

I have seen grace even in sorrow. I am always saddened when a fellow believer thinks, "God wanted such and such to happen to me," or "God is punishing me by letting me be sick," or any other such nonsense. Please hear me: *God is the one who is gracing you with the strength to make it through such seasons!* His grace got me through tremendous ups and downs and disappointments in the music industry. His grace got me through nearly losing my husband to meningitis—twice! His grace got me through the painful loss of a pregnancy. His grace got me through the death of my daddy. His grace is very, very real in times of sorrow. His grace. I live on it.

Grace and mercy are the reasons we have hope—and that is what everyone around us needs most. Have you noticed that? Today, more than ever, people are stuck in shame, fear, or confusion—their pits. The world is so full of buried dreams and broken faith that hope is difficult to see. What can we do about it? LOVE. Grace and mercy flow from the Father because He loves us! Did you know that neither life nor death, neither angels nor demons, neither the present nor the future, nor any powers, neither height nor depth nor anything else in all creation will be able to separate you from the love of God that is in Christ Jesus (Romans 8:38)? The most powerful thing you can do in this life is to show people *this* kind of love.

I have come to a point in my life where I am

sick and tired of the enemy and his plans for people. I will not allow the people I come in contact with to sit in their pits! Sorry, that means you too. When someone asks me for advice, I quickly pray that God will help me give a sweet dose of truth and wisdom that feels like love, grace, and mercy. Not the kind of sour truth bomb that hurts; there are already plenty of those being handed out by so-called "Christians." There, I said it. I know I mentioned this before, but if you have been the recipient of pain caused by the

Planting a Seed

No matter what mess you're in, what trouble surrounds you, or what stirs up negative emotions within you, His Word will bring healing.

Church, I want you to know something. *That is not who Jesus is.* He is love, grace, mercy, joy, peace—and truth. He is perfect. The Church is not. But you knew that already. You know why the Church isn't perfect? Because the Church is made up of people. People are messy.

I am going to go out on a limb here and assume that at some point, you have been lied to. You have been lied to by people, by Satan, and by people swayed by Satan. There have been things spoken over you that have brought destruction in

your identity and your purpose, and it's time you
fight back by speaking *life*. I don't know what truths
you are searching for right now, but I have a few that
everyone needs to hear:

> You are unconditionally loved by God.
>
> You were created in His image.
>
> You have a future and a hope.
>
> You are never alone.
>
> You are a sinner, just like me.
>
> You have a Savior, Jesus. He is the *only* way to
> eternal life.
>
> Your forgiveness was already purchased.
>
> Your peace has been provided for.
>
> You are precious to Him.
>
> You will never run out of grace and mercy
> from Him.

Beyond this short list of truths are a million
more for us to discover in the Bible. Now, don't check
out on me here. Maybe you've never given it much
thought, or maybe you've tried to discipline yourself
to read it every day so many times you're tired of fail-
ing at it. Here's the deal. No matter what mess you're
in, what trouble surrounds you, or what stirs up negative emotions within you, His Word will bring healing.

That's because His words are truth, and His truth brings freedom. Start small. Read the verse of the day on your phone or get a daily devotional that's full of quick one-pagers. (I am a little partial to the *At His Footstool* series, which I wrote. These are small devotional/dot journals, and they will get you going in the right direction if you have no idea how to begin. If you already have a devotional life, they'll bring a fresh new perspective. Start with the first one called *Bring Back Your Wow*.) Eventually, read the whole Bible. You can't imagine the clarity it will bring as you truly get to know GOD.

I know the truth can be scary when you are in the middle of making a mess of things! The truth can sometimes feel like a spotlight on your vulnerable nakedness. But guess what? Lies are even worse, because they literally put you under the leadership of the father of lies, the devil. And he wants to *devour you*. He wants to bind you up so tight that you give up ever hoping for true life. That is precisely where the devil wants you. Jesus scares the devil *because Jesus has already defeated him*. The devil doesn't want you to know that. The more he can keep you focused on all of your problems and all of your worries and all of your anxiety, the less chance there is that you'll over-come his control in your life. He hates Jesus, hates His grace and mercy for you, hates the love that over-comes everything because it also overcomes him! The reason the truth doesn't harm us when it comes from our God is that He is *love*–the perfect kind, and perfect love casts out fear (1 John 4:18).

Truth in love. Truth bathed in grace and mercy. Seek it and speak it. Even if it's uncomfortable at first. Don't stop. Fill your mind with truth from the Word, and there won't be room for lies. Light overcomes darkness, every single time. I'm praying for you right now. I pray that if you need truth to be spoken in your life, that you'll seek it, and that God will send the right people to speak it in love. I pray that if you need to speak the truth to someone, that the Holy Spirit will guide you to do so in the mercy and grace that only He can provide through His perfect love.

1 JOHN 4:18 (NLT)

Such love has no fear, because perfect love expels all fear. If we are afraid, it is for fear of punishment, and this shows that we have not fully experienced his perfect love.

DISCUSSION QUESTIONS

1. What are some of the gifts of mercy in your life?

2. Have you experienced grace in times of sorrow?

3. This chapter reminds us that Romans 8:38 says that neither life nor death, neither angels nor demons, neither the present nor the future, nor any powers, neither height nor depth nor anything else in all creation will be able to separate you from the love of God that is in Christ Jesus. Is there anything that you've assumed separates you from His love?

4. Of the list of truths, which one do you really need to cling to right now? Which one do you need to share with someone else?

5. Are you ready to commit to spending some time in the Word, so that truth can overtake the lies you've heard?

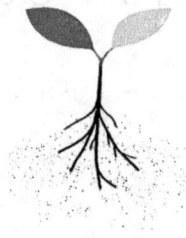

Beautiful Stillness

Be still. For some of us, it is almost impossible to stop moving unless we are sleeping . . . and some even move then! For others, we can still our body without a problem, but our minds are racing non-stop all the time. I've often related to the description of a mind that has too many tabs open all the time, like on a computer screen. If you've ever wondered why it's so hard to stop, listen, meditate, pray, sit in His presence, or in any way be still or quiet—here is your answer: *This world is uncontrollably loud.* It is harder than ever to ignore it . . . to get away from it . . . to just *be.*

In his book, *The Ruthless Elimination of Hurry,* John Mark Comer describes the era we live in where busyness and hurry are the norm. And they are killing us. Think about it; originally, man got up when the

Rebecca Frederick Lambert

sun rose and laid down to rest when it went down. At some point in the 1300s, the first public clock towers went up in Europe, and everything began to change as far as work schedules, sleep norms, and more. Fast forward to today, and most of us follow the schedule ordered by our alarm clock, not by whether our bodies have sufficiently rested. In elementary school, we learned that Thomas Edison invented the lightbulb in 1879. Did you know that before the lightbulb, people slept an average of ten hours a night? Today's average is seven. We live surrounded by an information download that is overwhelming, less-than-half-true, and constant. No wonder we are all tired; we are all feeling the urge to "keep up" while our soul *begs us to slow down*.

I'm not sharing this to discourage or overwhelm you. My hope is that this information helps you make sense of the anxious state of your heart and your desperate need for stillness. If you want to feel whole again as you dig out of that pit you've been stuck in, making time to be still before the Creator is absolutely necessary. Start small, and begin to see how even that little bit of time "away" transforms the way you see God, yourself, and the world around you. This is an area that I have to really work at, and probably always will. I have found that there are three basics to a beautiful time of stillness.

Be intentional. If even Jesus, who was God in the flesh, made time to get away with His Father, how can we think we don't need to? In Matthew 14, He went up on a mountainside. Where do you go? If you haven't tried intentional stillness before Him, this is your chance to plan it—where will you go? Is it somewhere that you can take in His creation? Is it just a quiet place? Is it far away or in your room? Wherever it is, you have to be intentional and go.

Be alone. That's the only way you will ever learn that you are never alone! Part of being alone is turning off every device. Man, being alone is just so hard to actually pull off these days!

It seems the world is pushing in all around us, clamoring for our attention. But I believe solitude needs to be a top priority for us as His followers. Jesus sought solitude with the Father; we need to do the same, and there is much

Planting a Seed

That little bit of time "away" transforms the way you see God, yourself, and the world around you.

strength to gain from it. Try it. Turn off *everything* and be alone with Him.

Be consumed. Let yourself get so wrapped up in Him that nothing else matters; not time, not tasks, not anyone else . . . just Him. When I see the way Jesus needed time away with His Father, I realize how far I am from the relationship I need to have with Him. I want to rely so fully on my Abba Father that I cannot go without my time away, fully consumed with Him. I liken it to when you are first dating someone and cannot wait to be together. That passion that burns for the other—that's how much you need God.

If all of this sounds impossible to do, just remember: The world will go on while you're "away." You will become more like you were intended to be. You will realize that He is enough. You will find strength in Him. Start small, and then make it a part of every day. In fact, now would be a great time! Mark your spot, and close this book. Sit still before Him for just two to five minutes. Let yourself breathe in His grace, His mercy, His love, and then breathe out any distractions, any worries, anything that isn't from Him. I'll be waiting for you here. (Go! Go!)

Even as you learn how to rest in Him, *you* might

need to be a "place of rest" for someone else. A place of safety. A refuge. I vividly remember certain parts of the crawl out of my pit. One thing that stands out to me is being welcomed to rest in the apartment of a college friend. She didn't even know me that well. I remember her making me ramen noodles and toast with a glass of milk. To this day, when I eat ramen, I recall that moment. Something that she has probably long forgotten by now was a gift to me: A place to rest, to fall apart if needed, to just be. God met me there. Are you willing to love someone in those simple ways? Because if you are, He will place opportunities in your path . . . be expecting it!

ZECHARIAH 2:13 (NLT)

Be silent before the Lord, all humanity, for he is springing into action from his holy dwelling.

DISCUSSION QUESTIONS

1. What are the things about your environment, this world, that you find *"uncontrollably loud"*?

2. Where do you or will you find quiet? If it's already a practice, how does it impact you? If not, what do you hope for?

3. Who do you know that might need you to be a place of refuge for them?

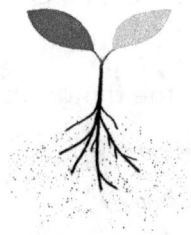

On Purpose

You're still with me in chapter seven! I feel like you and I are friends by now. You certainly know me pretty well, and you have given me some significant time to share my heart; thank you. I know the Holy Spirit is sitting right there with you as you read, just as I have known He is sitting with me as I write. I'm beyond grateful for that! Let's see what He does next.

If I had a dollar for each time I've heard, "I just want to know God's will for me," I'd be rich. We tend to make it so complicated; we worry that we might miss it, so we just stay put. Here's the deal. It's actually very simple, and it all stems from love. He wants the best for you, and His will *is* the best! Side note: If you are genuinely seeking God and His perfect will, He's not going to let you miss it. This chapter may feel a little like listening to a sermon on a Sunday, but I hope you'll find it's a good one!

When I think of God's will for us, our purpose as followers of Jesus, I think of the greatest commandment. In Matthew 22:37-39, Jesus declared, "'Love the LORD your God with all your heart and with all your soul and with all your mind.' This is the first and greatest commandment. And the second is like it: 'Love your neighbor as yourself.'" The first thing you need to know is that following Jesus means loving. Period. Notice, He tells us to love the Lord first, then others. I have learned from experience that it's because as we love God, and as we see how pure and wonderful His love is, we can't help but love others. And don't miss the part about loving others *as yourself*. There is a lot here, and it's okay to admit we haven't been great at any of these. Ask Him to help you!

I learned a lot about love as I watched my husband step into full-time ministry. Jesse's relationship with the Lord has continued to inspire me as he has prayed for the Lord to give him a heart for His people, and I have seen love pour out of this man for the countless people he ministers to around our city and everywhere he travels. He will actually tell you to be careful if you pray for God's heart, because it can be pretty painful. You might be moved to love people so deeply that you're willing to walk with them through really hard things. But it's worth it. When we really love people, it is not easy. It requires a lot of us, and it stretches us, and it's beautiful. That's how we grow to become more like Jesus. So, your first purpose is to love.

Second, you are not meant to do life alone. You were created to have a relationship with God and with other people. That looks like living a lifestyle of worship and building meaningful relationships with people. I've already mentioned that my happy place is singing to Jesus; I love to worship Him! But singing songs to Him will never fulfill me if I am not living a lifestyle that worships Him. Think about it this way: If someone tells you how wonderful you are, brings you gifts, tells everyone they know that you are amazing, and then turns around and acts like a jerk,

Planting a Seed

If you are genuinely seeking God and His perfect will, He's not going to let you miss it.

hurts people, lies, doesn't keep promises . . . wouldn't you want them to stop saying good things about you? Because in a way they'd be representing you . . . and you would rather not be associated with them. It's like having a "Jesus loves you" bumper sticker and then driving like no one else on the road matters. Man, sometimes it's better for us to be hidden away for a while to just spend time before Him and let Him transform us. When we worship Jesus, we let Him into our hearts; He doesn't just look at us on Sundays or any other time we sing to Him. How are we worshiping Him with our *everyday*?

Romans 12:1 says, "Therefore, I urge you, brothers and sisters, in view of God's mercy, to offer your bodies as a living sacrifice, holy and pleasing to God–this is your true and proper worship." Living sacrifice? Yes; your body is a temple, so take care of it. But it isn't meant to just be a nice temple, it's meant to *lay itself down in service to others*! That is an act of worship. Following Jesus means living as a sacrifice of worship to God the Father. We don't accidentally follow Him. We do so out of a response to His ridiculous love for us. We follow Him on purpose.

Like I mentioned before, the more we love God, the more we love people; therefore, all of our relationships will be more meaningful. Second

Corinthians 13:11 (NLT) exhorts us with these words: "Dear brothers and sisters, I close my letter with these last words: Be joyful. Grow to maturity. Encourage each other. Live in harmony and peace. Then the God of love and peace will be with you."

It's fun, encouraging, and plain ol' good for us to be with our family of believers. *And*, if we are learning from Jesus, we also need to be a "friend of sinners," right?

The church was never meant to be a club where you show off your Christianity! It was also never meant to be the one place you are willing to talk about Jesus and what He has done for you, and to worship Him. It's supposed to be a place where you learn and prepare for your purpose—but your purpose is *out there* in the world. Do you want to bring the light of Jesus to those around you at home, at work, at the store? Ask Him to help you love them well. Following Jesus means building relationships with others.

Next, let's look at Matthew 28:19-20. "Therefore go and make disciples of all nations, baptizing them in the name of the Father and of the Son and of the Holy Spirit, and teaching them to obey everything I have commanded you. And surely I am with you always, to the very end of the age." So . . . make disciples.

I know this verse may be familiar to some of you, but sometimes we brush right past the simple truth in it. This is a literal command from Jesus, so if you claim to follow Him, you should probably do it. Right? Be a disciple of Jesus and make disciples. What does that even mean? Well, a disciple is a student or follower; one who intentionally learns by inquiry and observation; one who studies. And *to disciple* means to teach, to train, to coach. Notice Jesus doesn't tell us to "therefore go and get people saved . . . " That would sure be a lot easier, wouldn't it? I can tell a whole bunch of people about Jesus and then move along to the next group, but that is not going to show them *how* to follow Jesus or how to be transformed and sanctified. We are called to live a life of training, teaching, and coaching others as they come into the Kingdom, to the point where they can do the same. This is a basic purpose for all followers of Jesus! We have really missed it . . . for a long time. I pray He gives us the strength and wisdom to do better.

Some of you are thinking, "Um . . . I'm not even getting it right *being* the disciple; how can I disciple someone else?" You don't have to have it all together to do it. In school, teachers know that if a student doesn't understand something, they should get another student to explain or model it for them. That goes a long way, even if the student modeling isn't perfect at it. So what I'm saying is that you can lead while you follow. Obviously, none of us are going to "arrive" and be done learning from Jesus, so if you keep waiting until you're "there," you will miss the chance to impact the lives of others. In fact, you'll never outgrow the need to be discipled or mentored. If we walk this out in humility, it will be okay when we make mistakes. Not only will we learn from them, but if we live out vulnerability, those following us closely will too!

At the end of the day, we need to *be* disciples and *do* discipling. How are you intentionally learning about Jesus by inquiring and observing? How are you studying Him and His life? Who are you discipling? Who has He placed in your sphere of influence, and what are you doing with them? Following Jesus means a life of discipleship.

Living life on purpose. Following Jesus on purpose. Loving, worshiping, building relationships, discipling . . . but really, it's all just loving. When you love, you live out Jesus. And you are right, it isn't always going to be easy. In fact, can I tell you something hard because I think I ought to? As a true follower of Jesus, you will disappoint people. Some may not understand your "new self," and they might not all accept you. It sounds crazy, but the truth is, people prefer that you stay with them in their misery. This is tough: Some of you have been "sharing a pit" with others who aren't ready to get out like you are. As painful and heavy as it is, you will have to leave them behind. However, I believe that as you allow God to move in your life, they will see your transformation and will want what you have.

I want to pause here and have you ponder with me this idea of being in that pit. When we are aligned with the will of the Father, He will use that pit for our good. There is a verse in Romans 8:28 that says, "And we know that all things work together for good to those who love God, to those who are called according to His purpose." Sometimes it is hard for us to see how He will bring good out of our situations. Whether we choose them or they fall on us, He does bring good. Sometimes the good He brings is for you, but sometimes it's for someone else.

Look at a seed planted in its little pit. This process brings benefits to the seed that eventually support its growth. The fact that it is underground allows it to keep its moisture. It is in the environment it needs to thrive. Another benefit of being underground is that no matter which direction its roots begin to sprout, it will be okay. It has freedom to grow in its own way. It's also hidden, where predators cannot get to it during this process. That gives it the time it needs. Being buried also keeps the seed in its place. I believe God can use your pit as a safe haven for you if you allow His presence to become the environment. He doesn't want to change who you are—He created you! He simply wants to give you the space to grow into more of what He has for you. He offers you a refuge from the enemy and gives you the time

Planting a Seed

Contrary to popular practice, being a Christian means you actually follow Jesus.

you need to grieve, let go, repent, and do whatever else you need to do. All the while, He keeps you in His view, holds you in His hand, right where you need to be. Will you surrender and let Him use your pit?

Listen, contrary to popular practice, being a Christian means you *actually follow Jesus*. It's not a one-and-done type of thing. It's a choice you make every single day to live your life the way He would have you live it. And what I want you to hear right now is that *your free will, your decisions, can either welcome God to move in your life, or limit Him in your life*. You can stay stuck where you are, or you can say yes to what He has for you. The enemy likes very much for you to stay stuck in your pit, believing you've blown it, and keeping God out of it because you're ashamed. The enemy wants you to believe you gave up your God-ordained purpose when you did (*fill in the blank*). This is a lie from the father of lies.

After Jesus died, the disciples, who were surely distraught, had returned to fishing because they knew it well and were comfortable there. When you fail, face disappointment, or run out of steam, you tend to do things that are comfortable and that keep you busy because you are afraid of what God is asking of you. But see? Those other things simply won't fulfill you because they are not *your purpose*. These disciples who actually walked with Jesus went back to what they knew because it was familiar. The disciples were meant to be fishers of *men*, not of fish. And you are meant to *thrive*, not just survive.

Have you noticed how many people are walking through life totally depressed? Many of them Christians. You are supposed to be following Jesus and leading others, not hiding. You are meant to powerfully burst out of that pit like an amazing, bold, beautiful plant that dances in the breeze of His Spirit and sheds seeds of love, joy, peace, and salvation! You are to be set up high to shine His light. And guess what? If there is something you aren't doing that *God straight-up created you for*, of course you are going to be depressed! Don't stay there! Let Him change everything as He leads you into purpose and ridiculous joy. Be obedient to Him, tell the devil to flee in the name of Jesus, and go. *You aren't going to live an exciting life for Jesus by accident. You have to do it on purpose.*

I see you, friend. I see you looking up, wondering if maybe it is time to reach out to Him; maybe it's time to trust that the One who created you did so on purpose and that He can show you the way. I can see you completely *unstuck*, laughing with joy, running toward the very plans that will bring you fulfillment.

Will you pray this with me? Pray it out loud: Holy Spirit, I invite You to move within me right now. Let these truths take root in my heart. Soak me in Your love. Thank You for restoring me, not to my original state, but to something even better. Help me when my faith is weak. Remind my soul that You know me so well and love me so well. I bind the lies of the enemy in the powerful name of Jesus Christ. I declare a restoration of my purpose.

PSALM 139:1–6 (TPT)

Lord, you know everything there is to know about me. You perceive every movement of my heart and soul, and you understand my every thought before it even enters my mind. You are so intimately aware of me, Lord. You read my heart like an open book and you know all the words I'm about to speak before I even start a sentence! You know every step I will take before my journey even begins. You've gone into my future to prepare the way, and in kindness you follow behind me to spare me from the harm of my past. You have laid your hand on me! This is just too wonderful, deep, and incomprehensible! Your understanding of me brings me wonder and strength.

DISCUSSION QUESTIONS

1. Is there someone or a group in particular that you struggle to love? Why do you think that is?

2. Who are the other believers you are doing life with?

3. How do you worship Jesus outside of a church service?

4. How can you bring the light of Jesus to those you do life around?

5. Is there anything you've returned to, because it was familiar, that you know won't fulfill you?

6. Is He speaking to you right now? Is He asking you to do something specific?

Worry for Worship

At times in my life, I've experienced spiritual "aha" moments. Especially when my academic background, emotional health, and spiritual searching all seem to align toward a single answer, those "light bulbs" tend to catapult me into a new season. I want to talk about one of those, and I know that as you allow Him to speak to you through these next few pages, you will find yourself pushing up and out of what's still keeping you in your pit.

Something that has been keeping people from bursting out of their pits and moving forward in their purpose for a long, long time is worry. The 2024 results of the American Psychiatric Association's annual mental health poll show that U.S. adults are feeling increasingly anxious. In 2024, 43% of adults said they felt more anxious than they did the previous year, up from 37% in 2023 and 32% in 2022. I cannot let you go back out into the world without giving you some tools to combat that.

To worry is to give way to anxiety or unease; it's allowing your mind to dwell on difficulty or troubles. Worry is a state of anxiety and uncertainty. The truth is that, although sometimes we worry about actual problems, we waste a lot of energy worrying about *potential* problems. When you look at the root word, you learn that it comes from the Old English *wyrgan*, which originally meant "to strangle." The use of the word changed over the years, first to mean "to harass," and then "to cause anxiety to." Wow. Is *wyrgan* something you want to be okay with?

Worry happens in your mind; it is defined as a repeated experience of thoughts about a potential negative outcome. Worry attacks your nervous system, brings tension to your muscles, and messes with your breathing and your heart's rhythm. This all leads to inflammation of blood vessels, which can lead to hardened artery walls and unhealthy cholesterol levels. The stress hormones produced when you worry give you a burst of blood sugar (meant to give you the energy to run if you're being chased by a grizzly bear), but if you're just sitting there worrying, you don't use that blood sugar. Storing it for too long can cause heart disease, strokes, or kidney disease. Your immune system is compromised, your stomach doesn't process properly, affecting your intestines, and the list goes on and on.

Can we all agree that worry is *bad*? It takes so much from us. I have had to come to the place of repentance over this—multiple times. I had to recognize that my worry was actually a sinful expression of my fear. It was affecting everything I did and everyone I loved, but mostly, it was robbing me of being me!

Planting a Seed
I had to recognize that my worry was actually a sinful expression of my fear.

For a long time, it had depleted my creativity. Because my mind was so busy worrying, it couldn't do anything else. So why repent? My worry was demonstrating a lack of faith in God, and more specifically, a lack of trust in God's love. See? Our worry implies that we think God doesn't really care about our needs.

I know the opposite to be true. First Peter 5:6-8

says, "Humble yourselves, therefore, under God's mighty hand, that he may lift you up in due time. Cast all your anxiety on him because he cares for you. Be alert and of sober mind. Your enemy the devil prowls around like a roaring lion looking for someone to devour." When you allow your thoughts to continually go toward fear, you are giving room for the devil to devour who you are . . . who you were created to be.

Novelist and playwright Arthur Somers Roche said, "Worry is a thin stream of fear trickling through the mind. *If encouraged*, it cuts a channel into which all other thoughts are drained." The devil wants exactly this! HE ENCOURAGES IT. If he can get our thoughts, he has us. I'm not talking about theoretical channels here; I'm telling you these thoughts create legit ruts in your brain. Scientists call these *ingrained neural pathways*. Call it what you will, it's up to you to declare the opposite of fear over your mind.

Second Timothy 1:6-7 (NKJV) tells us, "Therefore I remind you to stir up the gift of God which is in you through the laying on of my hands. For God has not given us a spirit of fear, but of power and of love and of a sound mind." This is one of the verses I would encourage you to memorize if you haven't already—and SAY IT out loud every time your mind tries to take you on the fear route. *This* is how we stop going down those same channels of fear. God has not given us a spirit of fear, but of power and of love and of a sound mind!

There is so much work being done in the arena of psychology to help people heal from habits of worry, fear, and anxiety. They call it "rewiring your brain." It is based on neuroplasticity (the brain's ability to adapt and create new pathways and connections). I find all of this fascinating. What excites me most is the fact that the things they've more recently "discovered" through their studies, the Word has been teaching us for thousands of years! See, our CREATOR knows how we work! (Ya think?) In Romans, He tells us that we can be transformed by the renewing of our minds (12:2). There are some amazing scientists that are gifted in their work, but He knows better than all of them about neuroplasticity . . . He came up with it!

The Bible has a whole lot to say about worry, and I encourage you to dig into all of it, but for now, I want to give you three tools to smash worry with. First, trust God completely. If you don't really know Him yet, you aren't ready to trust Him; so you may need to start there. This can look like reading the Word, praying, just making time to sit and listen. Here are three verses to get you started:

Proverbs 3:5-6 (NKJV) "Trust in the LORD with all your heart, and lean not on your own understanding; in all your ways acknowledge Him, and He shall direct your paths."

Philippians 4:6-7 (NKJV) "Be anxious for nothing, but in everything by prayer and supplication, with thanksgiving, let your requests be made known to God; and the peace of God, which transcends all understanding, will guard your hearts and your minds in Christ Jesus."

Psalm 56:3 (NKJV) "Whenever I am afraid, I will trust in You."

The second tool to smash worry with is to look up. This can be spending time in worship, telling Him what you're thankful for, and generally, setting your mind on Heaven. Here are my favorite verses for this tool:

Philippians 4:8 (NIV) "Finally, brothers and sisters, whatever is true, whatever is noble, whatever is right, whatever is pure, whatever is lovely, whatever is admirable—if anything is excellent or praiseworthy—think about such things."

Colossians 3:1-2 (NIV) "Since, then, you have been raised with Christ, set your hearts on things above, where Christ is, seated at the right hand of God. Set your minds on things above, not on earthly things."

Psalm 94:19 (NKJV) "In the multitude of my anxieties within me, Your comforts delight my soul."

Finally, the third tool you can use to smash worry is to put the work of the Kingdom first. This one isn't easy, because it's about humility. Put His mission before you and your needs, and put others first. The more you do it, the easier it gets. Trust in this verse:

First Peter 5:6-7 (NKJV) "Therefore humble yourselves under the mighty hand of God, that He may exalt you in due time, casting all your care upon Him, for He cares for you."

So to recap, trust in Him, look up, and put the Kingdom first. If you work on these, you will defeat worry. It's definitely worth the work.

I read this story and couldn't end this chapter without sharing it with you:

Years ago, when aviation was still being pioneered, a pilot was making a flight around the world.

He had certain fields set up for landing along the way; there were no official runways or landing strips yet. He was about two hours from his last field, and he heard a noise in his plane. He recognized the sound; it was the gnawing of a rat. It must have gotten on the plane while it was on the ground. For all he knew, the rat could be gnawing through a vital cable or control for the plane. It was a very serious situation, and he was worried!

At first, he didn't know what to do; he was two hours from the last field and two hours from the next. He was starting to panic. Then he remembered that a rat is a rodent. A rodent isn't made for heights; it's made to live on the ground, and even underground. So the pilot began to climb. He went up a thousand feet, then another thousand and another until he was more than twenty thousand feet up. The gnawing stopped. The rat was dead. He couldn't survive the

Planting a Seed

WORRY IS A RODENT. It cannot live in the secret place of the Most High.

atmosphere of those heights. More than two hours later, the pilot landed safely in the next field and found the dead rat.

WORRY IS A RODENT. It cannot live in the secret place of the Most High. It cannot breathe in the atmosphere of prayer and Scripture.

Jeremiah 17:7-8 (NKJV) "Blessed is the man who trusts in the LORD, and whose hope is the LORD. For he shall be like a tree planted by the waters, which spreads out its roots by the river, and will not fear when heat comes; but its leaf will be green, and will not be anxious in the year of drought, nor will cease from yielding fruit."

I want to be that tree! I want to be so rooted in God, so secure in Him, that nothing can shake me. I'm sure you want that too. If that's true, I encourage you to tell Him right now. Go ahead and confess the things you have been allowing to strangle you; the worries that have been harassing you because you weren't giving them to Him. And then let them go!

For a long time, I was carrying a lot of my own worries. The embarrassing part is that I was so sure of myself and my abilities that I didn't stop there; I was also carrying the worries and cares of many others! I felt like I had to shoulder the cares of people I led, people I cared about, people I read about on social media, people I heard about . . . Yes, it was ridiculous, and it was taking its toll on me physically, emotionally, and spiritually. A few years in, I had gotten away with some dear friends to spend some intentional time together and with God. One night, we were praying for one another, and God very clearly showed one of the ladies what was weighing on me. She saw me holding a hamper full of "cares." She also knew that many of them weren't even my own. She told me that God wanted me to put the hamper down. She said it was okay to bring the different cares to His attention, maybe stopping by to hold up one of them and pray, but I was not to pick the hamper back up.

I can't fully explain what happened that night, but what I can tell you is that I made a decision then and there. I said yes to what felt like God's command, and I left the hamper there. I felt lighter than ever and was truly elated! On top of that, it was like a switch was flipped; my old creative self suddenly came back to life within me, and I was ready to write, sing, and play for His glory. This book is a product of that decision!

Your *worry dies* when you ascend to the Lord's presence through trust, through prayer, through His Word, through worship, through humility. Whatever you're carrying, please put it down. Let Him take care of it. When you control the outcome, He cannot, and I can say from experience that His way is better.

JOHN 14:27 (NKJV)

Peace I leave with you, My peace I give to you; not as the world gives do I give to you. Let not your heart be troubled, neither let it be afraid.

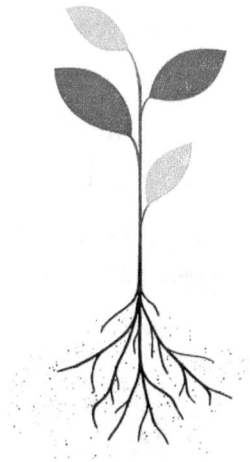

DISCUSSION QUESTIONS

1. This chapter shared that worry is the Old English word *wyrgan*, which originally meant "to strangle." The use of the word changed over the years first to mean "to harass," and then "to cause anxiety to." How does knowing this change your perspective on worry?

2. What are the things you tend to worry about?

3. Which of the Bible verses shared in this chapter will you memorize first?

4. Has worry been the thing that has kept you in a pit? Are you ready to repurpose that time you wasted on worry and use it for your purpose instead?

Prepare

PREpare: To make ready; to be willing to do something, like "I was prepared to do whatever it took to . . . " Preparing isn't always fun. Preparing usually means WORK. Think about an athlete preparing for a season or the big game, a runner preparing for a marathon . . . if they don't do the work beforehand, they probably won't succeed when the time comes. They say the game isn't won on game day—it's won in the work beforehand. Have you ever prepared something fun like a big Thanksgiving meal? There is so much work that has to happen to pull it off, from carefully choosing the ingredients to getting all the food hot and ready at the same time. The list goes on and on when it comes to things we have to prepare for . . . college tests, theater productions, new positions at work, welcoming a baby, traveling, and writing books! Psalm 27:14 (TPT) "Here's what I've learned through it all: *Don't give up*; don't be impatient; be entwined as one with the Lord. Be brave and courageous, and never lose hope. Yes, keep on waiting—*for he will never disappoint you!*"

You may be wondering why I am including a verse about WAITING when I'm talking about preparation, or equipping yourself for purpose. The truth is that what feels like a never-ending season of waiting is usually a season of preparation. After all, that prefix *PRE* in *pre*paration tells us that it happens BEFORE. So we have to be able to wait for whatever we are preparing for. Being able to wait requires faith. "Now faith is the substance of things hoped for, the evidence of things not seen" Hebrews 11:1 (NKJV).

We have the unfortunate challenge that we can't *see* Heaven right now . . . we can't see all that is going on in the spiritual realm around us (although you might have to be living under a rock to miss the fact that there is a *lot* happening). And your faith in His Word, in His promises, lets you know that He is with you, He has a plan for you, and that He will be faithful to complete the work He began in you! Faith is hard because what we *do see* is the chaos that surrounds us physically. So, guess what? We also have to prepare or train our minds if we want to do what God is asking of us. Romans 12:2 (NKJV): "And do not be conformed to this world, but be transformed by the renewing of your mind, that you may prove what *is* that good and acceptable and perfect will of God."

My question is, do you *want* to do what God is calling you to do? Are you willing to do what it takes to be ready? And how do you even prepare for your purpose? For His will? For His calling? By staying in relationship with your Abba Father. *No matter what.*

For Jesse and I, our prayer for our kids is that, no matter what mess they may end up getting themselves into, they will feel safe to come to us with it. Most parents would love their kids through anything! Our Heavenly Father is much better at loving us than we are at loving our kids. Just stay in relationship with Him. *No matter what.*

Look at David. Unfortunately, at one point, he put his own desires above God's. When we do that, we effectively remove Him from the throne of our lives. We no longer honor Him as our King. That is dangerous ground. For David, it was dangerous enough that it allowed him to lust after another man's wife, take her as his own, and then devise a terrible plan to kill her husband by sending him to the front lines in battle. David had disassociated himself from God. Maybe you are there right now. Have you allowed other things to take precedence over your relationship with Him? If you're there—I want to say, I'm so sorry. There is nothing more painful than being separated from God. There is hope. There is always hope.

We were created to have a relationship with God, and when that relationship becomes broken, our spirit is broken. It doesn't always come with outward evidence, but our spirit is truly grieved. We tend to bury ourselves in our shame and guilt. We confine ourselves to loneliness, afraid of stepping into light . . . afraid of who will be revealed! So, then what? David had certainly hit rock bottom. When the prophet Nathan called him out after David had committed adultery with Bathsheba, look at what David wrote in Psalm 51:10-12:

Planting a Seed

The truth is that what feels like a never-ending season of waiting is usually a season of preparation.

"Create in me a pure heart, O God, and renew a

steadfast spirit within me. Do not cast me from your presence or take your Holy Spirit from me. Restore me to the joy of your salvation and grant me a willing spirit to sustain me."

Do you see what David did? He ran back to God! He repented again. He made himself super vulnerable and asked for forgiveness. And then David went on to tell God that he would serve Him, tell of His great mercy, and worship Him. He ran back to God and once again declared Him his King. Today, we still call David "a man after God's own heart!" Not bad, huh? Just stay in relationship with Him.

Another way to be prepared for your future is to believe in who God says you are, and to remember He uses us in our weakness. I have seen so many times how He can use our greatest pain to fuel our best outpouring of love. Remember how hurt people will hurt people? Well, the opposite is also true; healed people will bring healing to people. We are really good at making excuses for why we aren't going after God's plan for our lives. And excuses are just that: a way to "excuse yourself" from doing what you should be doing. You might be thinking, "God, how can I tell people about you? I don't even follow you like I should. I don't know all the answers; I don't look like Jesus." We say to ourselves (with the help of the enemy who so readily affirms lies like: "Why would God use me when He can use her/him! He's/She's the type that God uses. I'm too (fill in the blank). I'm just not (blank) enough. Who am I that I should get to do that?" Or is that just me? Believe me, plenty of voices will tell you what you cannot do, who you will never be, and what you will never accomplish.

Those voices are *not* of our Father God. I'll give you one guess who those voices come from. You're right; often it's people who actually say the hurtful words. Some of you have experienced words of utter discouragement spoken over you by the very people who were supposed to lift you up. Some of you by your parents, siblings, other family, or friends. Some of you by pastors or teachers. Can I tell you something? They are not your enemy. Those people are simply the product of similar experiences they have not yet overcome. Satan is your enemy. People are not.

So what about when those ugly voices (or thoughts) come up? Second Corinthians 10:5: "We demolish arguments and every pretension that sets itself up against the knowledge of God, and we take

captive every thought to make it obedient to Christ."
When I think, "Oh, Lord—if I share my vulnerabilities
with a room full of people, they'll think I'm weak and
won't listen to me . . . " I take that thought captive and
make it obedient to Christ. Or, "Man, I really screwed
up this time. God could never forgive me . . . " I take
that thought captive and make it obedient to Christ.
How about, "No one really wants to be around me
unless they need something from me . . . " I take
that thought captive and make it obedient to Christ.
"I'm not smart enough . . . I'm alone . . . " I take that
thought captive and make it obedient to Christ!

You know what? When I finally got over myself
and the fact that I was embarrassed by the mistakes
I made early on in my adulthood (the ones that led
me into my pit), I was able to see how God could use
me in a powerful way to bring healing to others. Out
of my deepest pain has come my deepest desire
to bring life. I have
a voice that certain
people will listen to
because they know I

Planting a Seed

Just stay in relationship with
Him. No matter what.

get it. I get to speak truth because I've experienced
that truth. Maybe that's you. If I hadn't experienced

some of the intense disappointment I have, felt the
brokenness, or recognized my vulnerability, you
wouldn't give me room to talk. But I have, so you did.
That's how good God is. He can take your weakness
and make it a gift to someone else. Wait till you experience that joy!

Do you remember how important you are? First
John 3:1a (NKJV): "Behold what manner of love the
Father has bestowed on us, that we should be called
children of God!" John 15:15 (NKJV): "No longer do
I call you servants, for a servant does not know what
his master is doing; but I have called you friends, for
all things that I heard from My Father I have made
known to you." You are loved by the Creator of the
universe. He calls you His friend. Believe who He says
you are.

Next, surrender control to Him. Where you end,
He begins. Are you willing to follow Him beyond
"your end?" You have to trust Him for that. It's like
the old saying, "I'm at the end of my rope . . . " You
have to believe that His plan for you is better than
your own plan. Let go of the rope. You can't carry the
weight of what God wants to do, so don't try to. On
that note, quit trying to prove yourself by *doing more*.

In fact, I'm convinced more and more that our calling is much less about *doing* and much more about *being*. Let Him have control. It will be liberating!

Finally, prepare by being empowered. I have come to understand that empowerment is where skills meet permission. You have the skill set—we trust you to use that skill set for good. It dawned on me as I prepared to write this that as much as I agree with that definition, that kind of empowerment wouldn't be enough to fulfill my calling. Because that's where *my* skills meet permission. To obey His direction, what you will need is *supernatural* empowerment. That's where *His* skills meet not only permission from me, but the authority purchased for us by the blood of Jesus! Now that's empowerment! Acts 1:8 (NKJV): "But you shall receive power when the Holy Spirit has come upon you; and you shall be witnesses to Me in Jerusalem, and in all Judea and Samaria, and to the end of the earth."

As believers, we celebrate the greatest gift to humanity, Christ Jesus. He happens to be the ultimate example of being created for a purpose. His purpose was a beautiful gift for every one of us. It's wonderful to celebrate that on Christmas: His birth and the joy and hope He brings. So much about the history of His birth shows us how to prepare and live out our purpose. We can see it with Mary, Joseph, the Magi . . . in God the Father sending Jesus. And it gets a little harder when we begin to think about where Jesus would have to go from here . . . a life that was not easy, that was full of attacks from the enemy, plans of the religious people to make Him miserable—to destroy Him and His ministry—friends and family who doubted Him, close followers who denied and betrayed Him, and ultimately death on a cross. Heavy? Yes. Why am I bringing all of this up? Because Jesus, in the midst of all of that hardship, carried with Him a *joy* unspeakable, a *faith* that couldn't be shaken, a *love* that wouldn't budge, *grace* unfathomable, and a *peace* that we cannot truly understand to this day.

Let me tell you something that, for some time now, has continually blown my mind. You know that although Jesus was fully God, He was also every bit as human as us, right? Jesus had free will just like we do. Have you ever stopped to think that He had every right as a human to decide *not* to follow the Father's will? So many times, He could have chosen to avoid the discomfort, avoid the struggle, avoid the tough conversations . . . Even before going to the cross, in Matthew 26:39 (NKJV): He said to the Father: "O My Father, if it is possible, let this cup pass from Me; nevertheless, not as I will, but as You *will*." The TPT says it this way: "My Father, if there is any way you can deliver me from this suffering, please take it from me. Yet what I want is not important, for I only desire to fulfill your plan for me." He wanted to stay in relationship with you for all of eternity. *No matter what.*

It was His choice to submit to God's purpose, and further, to commit to preparing for it. It's ours too. What will you do?

1 PETER 1:13 (NIV)

Therefore, with minds that are alert and fully sober, set your hope on the grace to be brought to you when Jesus Christ is revealed at his coming.

DISCUSSION QUESTIONS

1. Is the idea of preparing for something new exciting or scary?

2. Have you ever felt like you were in a huge season of just waiting? Can you see ways in which you were being prepared during that time?

3. Have you allowed other things to take precedence over your relationship with Him? What do you need to do?

4. Are there thoughts on repeat that you need to take captive and make obedient to Christ?

5. What excuses have you used to "excuse yourself" from really following Jesus? In what ways do you need to surrender?

6. Have you ever asked God to empower you by His Spirit?

7. Will you submit to God's purpose, and further, commit to preparing for it?

Planted

I began this book with a graveyard of dreams. A place where people buried their hopes, desires, and their very identity under guilt, shame, and fear. I hope what you've read so far has brought you hope, love, and a reminder of the fact that you're so important as a unique creation of God. You were made by the Creator for significance. The Bible says that you are fearfully and wonderfully made, and even calls you His *masterpiece*! It also says that long before you were born, He planned good things for you. What you have inside of you is needed by someone else. The things you have gone through, as painful as they may be, can serve a purpose.

Back in 2002, as I began my own process of restoration and healing, I was starting to prepare for right now. It didn't seem like it at the time, and I just

thought I was "getting it together." I am not going
to sit here and tell you that the healing process I
walked through was easy. Oh no. I had to face a lot
of layers of stuff that I had hidden away for a long
time. And every time I thought I knew what it was that
God had been preparing me for . . . a surprise turn
would come. There were definite peaks and valleys,
moments of celebration, and seasons of extreme
pain. And guess what? He has never left my side.
He has always loved me through it, and little by little
I have learned to hear HIS voice over the voice of
others.

If you had told me in 2002 that God was preparing me to one day co-pastor a church and write books
that help bring healing and lead people to Jesus, I
really and truly would have laughed at you, and then
probably cried. But hour by hour, day by day, month
by month, and year by year . . . He has patiently led
me, healed me, and prepared me. All I had to do was
to stay close to Him, wait on Him, and obey Him. If
I could tell my "pre-restoration self" something that
would save me a lot of worry and anxiety, it would
be simple: "God really does love you more than you
can imagine. Relax." As I have reflected on the time

between leaving Argentina and today, I am over-
whelmed by everything God has brought me through.
As you now know, it hasn't always been easy, and I
have fallen flat on my face more than once, but one
thing is certain. He has been faithful, even when I
wasn't.

He wants to do the same for you. Hear me,
friend: God really does love you more than you
can imagine. Relax. He wants to walk through every
season with you. The ups and downs, the joy and the
sorrow, the successes and failures. All you have to do
is stay close to Him, wait on Him, obey Him. The life
ahead of you is truly an adventure.

I saw this "reel" in my mind that I want to share
with you. It was a beautiful day on a green hilltop, the
kind you imagine seeing in Ireland. There I was, and
you were there, too. We each had a jar, and for every
painful thing we had walked through, whether we
had a say in them or not, we received a seed, which
we put in the clear glass jar. The seeds began to
gather in the jars, creating very unique and interesting designs from the variety of colors, patterns, and
textures of the seeds. The design in each jar sort of
represented the person holding it. We each looked

at our jar, which had become strangely dear to us. I liked mine very much because it showed people some of what I had been through. I let it become a kind of trophy I was holding. You felt the same way about yours. Some of us carefully buried that jar in the ground, never to be bothered, keeping the seeds of our pain, disappointment, hurt, forever safe within the jar and underground.

The reel got more interesting when Jesus walked up. I watched Him. He would approach one person at a time and spend a moment talking, crying with them, holding their hands. I saw some of them sitting and crying, and some falling into Jesus' arms. Then I saw something more beautiful than I can describe with words. As Jesus spoke with one guy, he quickly dug up his jar. He turned it to look at it from every angle while tears streamed down his face.

Planting a Seed

What you have inside of you is needed by someone else.

Then, he took a deep breath and confidently handed it to Jesus. You won't believe what happened next. Jesus reached down, picked up a stone, and broke open the jar. Seeds flew out in every direction, and Jesus laughed with deep joy. The seeds landed all around us, and vibrant, giant flowers I have never seen before sprang up from the earth. The guy was laughing, spinning, spreading his arms out wide, and then we all realized what was happening.

Our seeds went from buried to planted when we handed them over to Jesus.

What He can do after that is beyond our understanding.

You have one of those jars.

Will you leave it buried, or will you dig it up and hand it to Him, trusting that He can do more with it than you can?

ISAIAH 61:1–3 (NIV)

The Spirit of the Sovereign Lord is on me, because the Lord has anointed me to proclaim good news to the poor. He has sent me to bind up the brokenhearted, to proclaim freedom for the captives and release from darkness for the prisoners, to proclaim the year of the Lord's favor and the day of vengeance of our God, to comfort all who mourn, and provide for those who grieve in Zion—to bestow on them a crown of beauty instead of ashes, the oil of joy instead of mourning, and a garment of praise instead of a spirit of despair. They will be called oaks of righteousness, a planting of the Lord for the display of his splendor.

DISCUSSION QUESTIONS

1. If you could tell your "in-the-pit" self anything, what would it be?

2. This chapter shared a "reel" about jars and seeds. What does it speak to your heart?

Epilogue

I hope joyful thoughts are etching their way through your mind. I hope in some way, you are feeling warm and fuzzy. I pray that you are filled with hope. Let's choose to have faith in a God who takes our pain, our failures, our weakness, and makes something really good out of it all. Romans 8:28: "And we know that in all things God works for the good of those who love him, who have been called according to his purpose." Those dreams, talents, desires He placed in your heart from the beginning have a divine purpose. It might take time, but let Him bring them back to life. Reclaim who you were created to be, and don't stop growing until you get to Heaven.

So, what now? Here are some things you can do

next. If your faith is still broken, follow someone very closely who is solidly following Jesus. Don't try to do it alone. If "church" is still a trigger word for you, ask God to heal you and direct you to the right place of worship so you can connect. People hurt you; Jesus did not. He never will. And beyond that, He completely understands your hesitation around religion. Religious people nailed Him to the cross. The truth is that you need Jesus, and you need people. I am praying right now that you will find your people.

Stand up and repent if you need to, then receive the outpouring of mercy and grace. It's soothing, it's healing, it's restoring, it's life-giving, it's beautiful. Nothing compares to the love we receive from the Father. No matter how long it takes us to come back to Him, He runs out to meet us and celebrates that we are home. Surrender to Jesus is the single most life-giving thing you can do. I guarantee it.

Plan a time and place to escape and just be in His presence. When you get there, ask Him to fill you up! Every day, get up and go on a mission to love people—it's fulfilling. When you find yourself worrying, worship instead. Find something worthy of doing, and prepare for it. He will show up in the process. And when you find yourself holding onto the past, the pain, the failures, remember to give that jar back to Jesus. He makes all things new.

And then? Well, if I say I am a "follower of Jesus," then I better be moving! The thing is that once we know the truths that the Bible teaches us, we are then responsible; we are accountable to them. Jesus didn't die a gruesome death on a cross so that we could sit comfortably knowing we would go to Heaven! We are to follow Him! And we are called to become "fishers of men." I am not going to mislead you; there is a price to pay in order to follow Jesus. An amazing poet and one of my teen idols said it this way: "I don't wanna gain the whole world and lose my soul." Thanks, TobyMac.

I have in no way come even close to "arriving," but the longer I live with the intent to walk in step with the Holy Spirit, the more I realize how short this earthly life is in comparison to eternity with Jesus. When you realize that life continues after we leave our earthly body, everything gets put in such a refreshing perspective. For example, when I hear someone say something like, "Well, I only have so much time left in my life, and there's still so much

I want to do . . . " I immediately want to say—"Well, you have all of eternity!" Maybe this life is just our practice. It's like the qualifying race before we go to Heaven and really join the A Team! It will cost us, but it will be worth every bit of that cost.

Listen, if what you're after in this life is a comfortable, clean, safe, organized, pretty little life all tied up with a bow, Jesus isn't the way. I'm just being real with you right now. A life of following Jesus is more like a spiritual Spartan race around the world. There will be trials. It will be so hard at times. But you are

Planting a Seed

Our seeds went from buried to planted when we handed them over to Jesus.

surrounded by a great cloud of witnesses cheering you on—because they know it's worth it. (I hear you, Daddy!)

It's time for you to take a step of faith, get a little uncomfortable, and move. It's time for you to be a little bold with your faith, even if you haven't figured it all out yet. What is that next step for you? Making it a priority to connect to a family of believers? Scheduling time to read the Word and actually get to know this man named Jesus? Maybe you're further ahead in your walk . . . is it time to prepare for something He's been talking to you about? Is He asking you to give up some part of your lifestyle so that you can be freed up to serve others? Listen to His voice; He is talking to you. He is pouring out a new thing. Will you receive it?

Today, I am a busy girl. I am the wife of an amazing man who believes in my huge ambitions and invests in me every day. I am a boy-mom to some charming, witty, and fun sons who already serve Jesus. I lead a staff of committed, creative, passionate, incredible educators who are changing lives each day. I co-pastor a church where we model authentic, repentant Christianity and where people find healing and restoration because they are loved first

Planting a Seed
Surrender to Jesus is the single most life-giving thing you can do. I guarantee it.

and then prepared for their calling. Every day, I sing with all my heart to the One who brought me back to life. And I write, because that is one of the dreams I had buried, and Jesus restored it.

People often ask me how in the world I keep up with everything and how I am so full of joy all the

111

time. I usually don't have an answer prepared, so I just laugh and brush it off. But what I'm thinking is, "If you only knew me in my darkest moment, you'd know the only way I could be who I am today is Jesus." So now you know. I grasp onto that new mercy every morning. I'm full of joy, energy, and love because He has restored me, and I am brand new. My roots run deep, and they soak up His Word, His Spirit every day. I gave it all to Jesus.

I'm not buried—I'm planted.

PSALM 30:11–12 (NIV)

You turned my wailing into dancing; you removed my sackcloth and clothed me with joy, that my heart may sing your praises and not be silent. Lord my God, I will praise you forever.

Thanks

At first, I thought that a small section of this book was totally unreasonable as an attempt to thank the people who need to be mentioned. I sat and pondered how to even start. Eventually, I realized that trying to list every name and every person that has impacted the words on these pages would end in underwhelm. So rather than trying to thank you all in a way that falls short, I'm going to be thankFUL for you in a way that I hope brings life.

I'm eternally thankful for the many gifts my Heavenly Father has given me. I am thankful for my church family at large (and boy, is it large) all over the world. From the church that began to raise me in Buenos Aires, to the one that loved me through the pain in Oklahoma, from Missouri to Tennessee, and

Texas . . . you have all remained in my heart. To The Refuge, Texas: Thank you for loving and supporting us in the busiest season of our lives. You are loved beyond measure. Keep leading others in authenticity and repentance as you follow Jesus, continually preparing for the full purpose the Lord has for each of you.

I'm thankful for the crazy obedience and submission of my parents, Michael and Lolita, to serve on the mission field and then in the USA, and for the way I was loved and raised in both settings. I am thankful for my sisters, Brenda, Leahna, and Debra, for being the most important role models in my life. My love and admiration for you is gigantic and only continues to grow. I'm thankful for my big "brothers," so carefully chosen by my sisters: Denny, Don, and Terry. You have no idea how much I love you and have looked up to you. I thank God for grandparents, aunts and uncles, cousins, nieces, and nephews, all who have had a beautiful impact on my life. I'm thankful for my bonus mama, my mother-in-law, Gwen, who has always loved me well (and spoiled me a lot), and for all of the Lambert family. I cherish each of you so much, and know God's plans are so good. I'm thankful for the surprise gift of a bonus dad, Steve, and for the grandfather you are to my sons: You are one of the many ways our Father has shown off for my mommy and my family.

Second to my salvation, the greatest gift of grace in my life is my marriage. Jesse, you first chose to love me while I was so broken, and we got to walk the road of restoration, healing, and growth together. You have supported me through each of my God-sized dreams, and you have never once given up on me. My delicate heart is held by your sweet love every day. You have taught me about sacrifice, true dedication, grit, adventure, and fierce commitment. You are my hero, and I love you deeply.

Asher and Gideon, you will forever be the joy in my heart. You make me immensely proud every day. Thank you for loving this mama so well and for believing that our family's ministry matters. You have served, you have sacrificed, and you have loved. I'm thankful for the memories we get to keep making together. You are each uniquely gifted and already carry so much authority in the Kingdom of Heaven. Never forget that you are royalty because of Jesus. I love you, boys.

And finally, I'm thankful for you, the reader. You chose to read this book all the way through, and I don't take that for granted. I believe the Holy Spirit has been moving in your heart as you have read, and I pray you will keep letting Him do just that. I hope our paths cross one day, if not here in this life, as we worship together in Heaven!

About the Author

Rebecca Lambert is a coach, speaker, church leader, wife, and boy mom. Known for her warmth and authenticity, she is passionate about loving people well and helping them walk in their God-given calling. A gifted worship leader and anointed writer, Rebecca lives what she teaches—modeling worship as a way of life and trusting God's redemptive work through every season. Whenever she has the microphone, she seeks to speak wisdom in the form of truth and love. Rebecca is co-pastor of The Refuge in Georgetown, TX, and a leader in her school district. She loves spending time with her husband, Jesse, and their two sons, Asher and Gideon.